Great African-Americans

W. E. B.
DU BOIS

by Jeni Wittrock

Content Consultant: Allen Ballard, Professor,
History and Africana Studies, University at Albany

Consulting Editor: Gail Saunders-Smith, PhD

CAPSTONE PRESS
a capstone imprint

Pebble Books are published by Capstone Press,
1710 Roe Crest Drive, North Mankato, Minnesota 56003
www.capstonepub.com

Library of Congress Cataloging-in-Publication Data
Wittrock, Jeni.
  W. E. B. Du Bois / by Jeni Wittrock.
    pages cm. — (Pebble books. Great African-Americans)
  Includes bibliographical references and index.
  Summary: "Simple text and photographs present the life of W. E. B. Du Bois, a scholar and civil
rights activist"—Provided by publisher.
  ISBN 978-1-4914-0505-5 (library binding) — ISBN 978-1-4914-0511-6 (pbk.) —
ISBN 978-1-4914-0517-8 (ebook pdf)
  1. Du Bois, W. E. B. (William Edward Burghardt), 1868–1963—Juvenile literature. 2. African
Americans—Biography—Juvenile literature. 3. African American intellectuals—Biography—Juvenile
literature. 4. African American civil rights workers—Biography—Juvenile literature. I. Title.
  E185.97.D73W554 2015
  323.092—dc23
  [B]   2014007342

Editorial Credits
Nikki Bruno Clapper, editor; Terri Poburka, designer; Kelly Garvin, media researcher;
Laura Manthe, production specialist

Photo Credits
Alamy Images: Michael Dwyer, 18; Corbis/Rick Friedman, 12; Getty Images, Inc: Archive Photos,
cover, 10, NBCUniversal, 20, The Life Picture Collection, 4; Glow Images: CSU Archives/Everett
Collection, 14, Everett Collection, 16; Print Collection Miriam and Ira D. Wallach Division of Art,
Prints and Photographs Division, The New York Public Library, Astor, Lenox and Tilden Foundation,
6, Photographs and Prints Division, The Schomberg Center for Research in Black Culture, The
New York Public Library, Astor, Lenox and Tilden Foundation, 8; Shutterstock/Sopotnicki, cover art

Note to Parents and Teachers

The Great African-Americans set supports national curriculum standards for
social studies related to people, places, and environments. This book describes and
illustrates W. E. B. Du Bois. The images support early readers in understanding
the text. The repetition of words and phrases helps early readers learn new words.
This book also introduces early readers to subject-specific vocabulary words, which
are defined in the Glossary section. Early readers may need assistance to read
some words and to use the Table of Contents, Glossary, Read More, Internet Sites,
Critical Thinking Using the Common Core, and Index sections of the book.

Printed in the United States of America in Stevens Point, Wisconsin.
032014   008092WZF14

Table of Contents

4

Meet W. E. B.

W. E. B. Du Bois

was a writer, teacher,

and leader. He fought for

equal rights and education

for African-Americans.

W. E. B. at age 4

Early Years

W. E. B. (William Edward Burghardt) Du Bois was born in Massachusetts in 1868. At that time many schools were segregated. But W. E. B.'s school had black and white students.

W. E. B. in his college days

1868 born

1884 graduates from high school

In 1884 W. E. B. graduated from high school at the top of his class. Then he went to college in Tennessee. He saw that blacks had to live apart from whites in the South.

1868
born

1884
graduates from
high school

W. E. B. thought life was
unfair for African-Americans.
He thought blacks and whites
should have the same chances.
Everyone deserved a try at the
best schools and jobs.

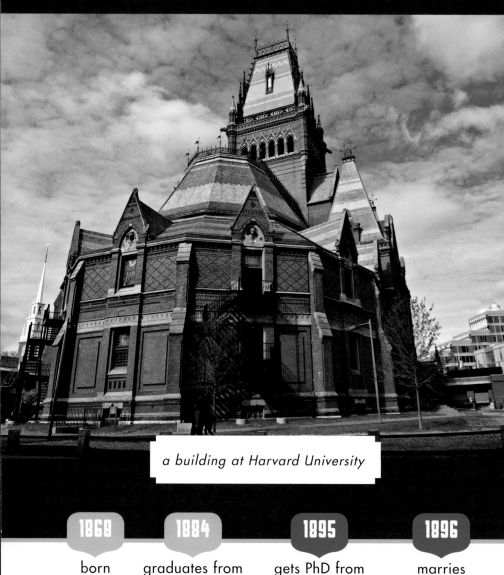

a building at Harvard University

1868
born

1884
graduates from
high school

1895
gets PhD from
Harvard University

1896
marries
Nina Gomer

As an Adult

In 1895 W. E. B. was
the first African-American
to get a PhD from Harvard
University. In 1896 he
married Nina Gomer.
They had two children.

1868
born

1884
graduates from
high school

1895
gets PhD from
Harvard University

1896
marries
Nina Gomer

W. E. B. became a college
teacher. He also wrote
books, articles, and poems.
His most famous book is called
The Souls of Black Folk.

W. E. B. (bottom row, third from left) at a meeting of the NAACP

1868	1884	1895	1896
born	graduates from high school	gets PhD from Harvard University	marries Nina Gomer

In 1909 W. E. B.

helped start a group

for African-Americans.

It was called the NAACP.

This group still helps

black people today.

1909

helps start
the NAACP

W. E. B.'s house
in Ghana, Africa

1868	1884	1895	1896
born	graduates from high school	gets PhD from Harvard University	marries Nina Gomer

Later Years

W. E. B. traveled around the world and shared his ideas. He spoke out for peace and equality. In 1959 W. E. B. received the Lenin Peace Prize. In 1961 he moved to Africa.

1909
helps start the NAACP

1959
receives Lenin Peace Prize

1961
moves to Africa

March on Washington in 1963

| **1868** | **1884** | **1895** | **1896** |
| born | graduates from high school | gets PhD from Harvard University | marries Nina Gomer |

W. E. B. died in 1963.

The next day 250,000 people

marched for African-American

rights in Washington, D.C.

They had a moment of

silence for W. E. B. Du Bois.

1909	1959	1961	1963
helps start the NAACP	receives Lenin Peace Prize	moves to Africa	dies

Glossary

article—a piece of writing in a newspaper or magazine

college—a school that students attend after high school

deserve—to earn something because of who you are or the way you act

graduate—to finish all the required classes at a school

equal—the same as something else in size, number, or value

equality—being equal

NAACP—National Association for the Advancement of Colored People; a large group of people who fight for equality for African-Americans and others

PhD—the highest degree you can earn at a university; when you have a PhD, people call you "Doctor"

right—something that everyone deserves

segregate—to keep people apart because of their skin color

Read More

Evans, Shane. *We March*. New York: Roaring Brook Press, 2012.

Jeffrey, Gary. *Medgar Evers and the NAACP. A Graphic History of the Civil Rights Movement*. New York: Gareth Stevens Publishing, 2012.

Pinkney, Andrea Davis. *Sit-In: How Four Friends Stood Up by Sitting Down*. New York: Little, Brown and Company, 2010.

Internet Sites

FactHound offers a safe, fun way to find Internet sites related to this book. All of the sites on FactHound have been researched by our staff.

Here's all you do:
Visit *www.facthound.com*
Type in this code: 9781491405055

Super-cool stuff!

Check out projects, games and lots more at
www.capstonekids.com

Critical Thinking Using the Common Core

1. How did W. E. B. want to make life better for African-Americans? (Key Ideas and Details)

2. What does it mean to respect a person? Why do you think people respected W. E. B.? (Craft and Structure)

Index

Word Count: 226
Grade: 1
Early-Intervention Level: 20